Diary of A Worshiper

A Devotional

My friend & Sis!

Always,
Caprichia

Caprichia Smith

DIARY OF A WORSHIPER: A DEVOTIONAL

© 2016 by Caprichia Smith

Books may be purchased, in quantity and/or special sales by contacting the author.

ISBN 978-1-945172-27-4

Prov31 Publishing (http://authorprenuer.net)

Printed in USA by A & R Printing (a-rprinting.com)

PREFACE

Diary of a Worshiper is an expression of confirmation for those struggling to respond to a calling to minister in a world where things are not simply black or white. It provides a realistic snapshot of the journey of one who is dedicated to upholding the mantle of Worshiper, as she discovers the other aspects of her ministerial gifts.

Psalmists, preachers, prophets, etc. prepare themselves in a variety of ways . . . God prepares these servants as diversely! In *Diary of a Worshiper*, the author shares excerpts of that preparation as recorded during her periods of journaling. The correlation of one's deliverance in an authentic practice of worship and devotional reflection is also emphasized within these entries.

The author suggests that the revelations that accompany this analysis provide both liberation and deliverance, when authentically exercised. In *Diary of a Worshiper*, the author explores this theory by encouraging the reader to begin or continue a journaling experience through this devotional format.

Standing or struggling . . . weeping tears of joy or pain, the author's confessions provide you, the reader, with the opportunity to find freedom in your individual story, righteousness in your private journey and celebration in your own personal testimony.

"For I know the plans I have for you, declares The Lord, plans to prosper you and not harm you, plans to give you hope and a future." (Jeremiah 29:11 NIV)

TABLE OF CONTENTS

FORWARD

So often, we have our own ideas about how our lives will look. When our lives do not turn out quite like we imagined, we are surprised and often get discouraged. We even attempt to determine if our lives have purpose at all, and if so, we go on a quest to identify it. With each new day, each new mercy and each new experience, our wisdom in these matters should increase. When we are fortunate enough to learn from these experiences, we can accept that the purpose of our lives was never in our control, anyway. Our maturity invites us to "… lay aside every weight, and the sin which so easily ensnares us, and let us run with endurance the race that is set before us, looking unto Jesus, the author and finisher of our faith, who for the joy that was set before Him endured the cross, despising the shame, and has sat down at the right hand of the throne of God." (Hebrews 12:1-2 NKJV)

We can only discover the true purpose of our lives through submission to God. Only then will we really know why we were created, specifically. Without this revelation, many spend all of their lives wondering if their real purpose will ever be revealed. When we agree to accept that God is in control and come to the realization that it was never about what we could plan or imagine in the first place, then we can benefit from the encouragement Paul penned to the Church at Corinth: "… Eye hath not seen, nor ear heard, neither have entered into the heart of man the things which God hath prepared for them that love Him." (1 Corinthians 2:9 KJ21)

Open your hearts and rediscover God's purpose for you through the life of one of His chosen as you read *Diary of a Worshiper*. In this book, Reverend C. invites us to grow with her through her struggles with identification, revelation, justification and validation. In this untainted, authentic journey, we can find the strength to discover our own place and purpose.

~ Courtney Michelle Davis

Purpose of a Worshiper

Dear Diary,

I'm Here! Swift delivery and increased anxiety yielded the second, 7-pound miracle. Ten fingers, ten toes, two eyes, tiny little nose . . . God had kept yet another promise. No name and no clear explanation of what the future of this little blessing would be . . . but here, nonetheless.

When your parents are committed to Christ, your life can be somewhat targeted. My parents didn't put that pressure on me. They walked upright before my siblings and me and allowed us to grow in faith at our own pace. I'm not sure if either of us really knew that I was set-apart to endure seasons of doubt, deliverance and despair . . . yet destined to see the glory of God unfold under the sound of my voice, the peace of my obedience or the provision of God's faithfulness.

I still reflect on how I got here and how faithful You have been all of these years, God. I've been privileged to dwell in Your presence and I know I don't deserve it. I'm grateful that You have endowed me with the determination to fulfill my purpose. I'm overwhelmed by the grace You've shown me, repeatedly . . . and although I have come to know that You have my steps ordered, honestly, I'm still nervous. I don't want to fail You or Your people. I don't want to take You or this anointing for granted. Yet, in the midst of all of my reservations, I hear you urging me to hear what You said to Jeremiah . . . so, all I have to do is just live!"

Focal Scripture: "Before I formed you in the womb, I knew you. Before you were born, I set you apart. I appointed you as a prophet to the nations." (Jeremiah 1:5 NIV)

Reflection: What is your God-given purpose? How do you overcome obstacles that seem insurmountable on your journey to fulfilling that divine purpose?

SACRED SPACE

_____

_____

_____

_____

_____

_____

_____

_____

_____

_____

_____

_____

_____

_____

_____

_____

_____

Dear Diary,

Restoration has finally come! My Spirit has been tossing all day. I keep hearing RESTORATION! This is a season of alignment meant to prepare the body of Christ for a period of warfare that is imminent. We are called into battle but we are chosen for victory! There's a lot of work to do to see that victory and I believe it begins with our complete restoration!

Through Your Son, the restoration of my relationship with You has nurtured my ability to hear from You, learn Your ways, and apply Your principles with integrity and humility. Being restored opens my heart to the plight of the chastised and disenfranchised. I now realize that You are raising up a generation who will advocate for the restoration of the Church's authority. Authority over the moral and ethical accountability of the world; so that those who are in the church are no longer simply mirror images (or worse) of the sin that plagues those who are outside of a covenant relationship with Christ!

I know that in You, we can live, love, hope, and be healed. I'm resting on the promises of a Savior who will go before us in battle. Reaping the harvest of true labor and authentic worship. Reviving the spiritually-dead and those who have been crippled by past pains. I'm interceding for the repentance of those who abandon the truth to pack pews, line their own pockets, and prostitute God's people! I'm watching You align all of the pieces and it's just reassuring to know that it will ALL WORK TOGETHER FOR OUR GOOD!!!

Focal Scripture: ". . . I will restore to you the years that the swarming locust has eaten . . ." (Joel 2:23-27 ESV)

Reflection: What are the dreams on which you are you resting? What motivates you to keep pressing when life's challenges are distracting?

SACRED SPACE

_____

_____

_____

_____

_____

_____

_____

_____

_____

_____

_____

_____

_____

_____

_____

_____

_____

_____

_____

Dear Diary,

I am having a "come-to-Jesus" moment . . . Yet, I still hear you calling me to listen! I have to share this word with someone and I'm not sure how it will be received. I guess I'll just tell it like it is . . . When the enemy comes against you, you cannot allow him to condemn you or make you doubt your intentions! God does not operate like this! It's actually quite the opposite! You must be doing something right! Satan is the Father of Lies . . . So, he succeeded in distracting the joys of unity, bonds of family, and hope for a peaceful future. But we cannot walk away allowing Satan to have the last say. You did nothing wrong. . . So your response to these lying, backbiting, gossiping agents of Satan should be 'Get Thee behind Me, Satan!'

Why would you be bound to the lies others are spreading about you? Why would you allow yourself to be held down and depressed by the vicious tricks of the enemy? This is when our faith should kick into overdrive! They CAN'T have your peace unless you give it to them. They CAN'T have your joy unless you hand it over to them. They CAN'T overpower you, kill you, or even damage you without your permission!!! Jesus told Pilot, *"The only power you have is what My Father gives you!!!"* And I decree that NO WEAPON FORMED AGAINST YOU SHALL PROSPER!!!

Be bold and strong in The Lord and the power of His might. Rise up and live in the privilege that has been bestowed to you by Our Father!! Walk in the reassurance that God has a plan for all of this to work together for your good!!!

Focal Scripture: "And we know that in all things God works for the good of those who love Him, who have been called according to His purpose." (Romans 8:28 NIV)

Reflection: How do you handle moments of false accusation? How do you overcome them?

SACRED SPACE

_____

_____

_____

_____

_____

_____

_____

_____

_____

_____

_____

_____

_____

_____

_____

_____

_____

Dear Diary,

Miracles seemed impossible and then this little, 6lb, 9oz heart throb arrived. He has been tugging at my heart strings ever since. His inquisitiveness, strength for subtle discovery, willingness to explore every possibility, and unyielding desire to love without barriers serves as proof that God still uses miracles to enhance our faith and foster our future! His heart for people is reassuring and his quest to understand the things of God reminds me that his perception and identity are already being matured. Kevin III . . . The miracle of your life and innocent witness continues to be a blessing to me! This child will have my heart, forever. Kevin, Momma loves you, endlessly!

Even at such a young age, Caleb has taught me so much. He approaches new situations with fervor and deliberate effectiveness . . . traits that keep me on my toes. Challenges are only temporary for Caleb . . . he rises to the occasion each and every time with undeniable confidence that guides his next endeavor. His "Super Hero" alter ego is definitely true to form. Through his life, his quest to be a blessing, even now, his inquisitive mind, determined attitude and his therapeutic, healing touch...Caleb is destined for greatness! This child will forever have a unique part of my heart. Caleb, Momma loves you, infinitely!

As I celebrate the blessing that has been motherhood, I embrace the lessons that raising anointed children have granted me. God has shown me so much favor in the rearing of my healthy, handsome, gifted, and chosen Kings in Training! My heart skips a beat every time I see them smile and feel their warm, adoring touches . . . their affection is infectious and their existence reminds me just how much God loves me.

Being their mother has cured me from hopelessness and renewed my faith in humanity! My babies teach me to live on purpose. They help me see past my inefficiencies and perpetual lack to the provision that has been established in the grace that God ordains each and every day. The perceived fate of condemnation for those conceived by two but nurtured by only one, pales in comparison to the glory that shall be revealed in the latter days for those who have been thrust into these neglectful dilemmas beyond their control. These children are chosen and focused, already. They are God's fullness of joy in the flesh. Thank you, Lord, for trusting me with their lives and livelihood.

It takes a village to raise our children, and I thank God for the Villagers who have sown into the lives of my babies. Especially since we live in a world where tradition is now viewed in trepidation, conception is now a consequence and both responsibility and religion are considered cliché. In a society in which everything seems to be awry, my budding Kings find their rightful place beyond my bosom. They plant their feet on the platform of their destiny and they live their lives on purpose - - - with purpose - - - and for a purpose!

Focal Scripture: "I thank my God upon all my remembrance of you, always in every supplication of mine on behalf of you all making my supplication with joy, for your fellowship in furtherance of the gospel from the first day until now; being confident of this very thing, that he who began a good work in you will perfect it until the day of Jesus Christ." (Philippians 1:3-6 ASV)

Reflection: Review "Grateful" by Hezekiah Walker. If you could, list all of the things, people, conditions, etc. that make you grateful. Good luck!

SACRED SPACE

Dear Diary,

Authenticity is hard to hide! Today was wild. So, I'm grateful for this release. It reminds me of the times I spent growing up with my big sister. CoCo invested in me. Since I could remember, she was my role model and confidant. Even as a child, I attempted to walk like her (though her bowed legs were hard to imitate). I tried to talk like her (. . . *my conversational prowess is strongly attributed to the patience she exemplified when helping me say words, correctly)*. I even wanted to dress like her; because of our age difference, I looked forward to wearing clothes that I learned had belonged to her.

For some reason, though, CoCo's shoes never seemed to fit me. They were too narrow, too something . . . the shoes just wouldn't work. Figuratively, I guess I never quite got the same fit, either. I just never learned to fill her shoes with the grace, skill, and diligence that she did in the face of adversity. She was a warrior and a hero all rolled into one. As supernatural as she seemed to me, her genuine concern for the wellness of others was never sacrificed.

It was the relationship with my CoCo that taught me the importance of meeting people where they are. CoCo helped me find the good in people and taught me how to intercede for those in whom that good was a little harder to find. My big sister was my first pastor, my first teacher and my first mentor. She was my first friend . . . and that was exactly what I needed.

Focal Scripture: "My intercessor is my friend as my eyes pour out tears to God; on behalf of a man, He pleads with God as one pleads for a friend." (Job 16:20-21 NIV)

Reflection: What relationships brought you to the realization of your complete self? What values make you unique to the Kingdom of God?

SACRED SPACE

_____

_____

_____

_____

_____

_____

_____

_____

_____

_____

_____

_____

_____

_____

_____

_____

_____

Dear Diary,

Today, my heart stopped. When I got the call that Daddy never showed up at the funeral where he agreed to sing, I knew something strange had happened. No risks, no warnings … yet, Stroke just came in and got comfortable. Well, I'm a Daddy's girl and whatever I ask in prayer in faith, shall be done (Matthew 21:22), so Stroke, I rebuke you and counteract your damages with The Blood of Jesus.

In the Name of Jesus, I command my Daddy's tongue to realign itself so that the words are clearer than ever before. I command the brain cells to regenerate in the Name of Jesus so that the elements of speech that were affected are healed, completely. I command the memories of joy and hope to be restored, expeditiously, as if it were all just a bad dream. I command the eyes to line up into 20/20 vision. I command the songs of praise in his heart to spring forth like a flood with greater anointing than ever before. I speak restoration of harmony, melody, syncopation, theological accuracy and spiritual revelation for my Daddy in the Name of Jesus. Christ was wounded for our transgressions. He was bruised for our iniquities. The chastisement of our peace was upon Him, and so I decree that by His stripes, my Daddy is healed. (Isaiah 53:5) And Daddy, I'm going to believe it for you until you can find the hope and faith to believe it for yourself!

Focal Scripture: "Then shall thy light break forth as the morning, and thy healing shall spring forth speedily; and thy righteousness shall go before thee; the glory of Jehovah shall by thy reward." (Isaiah 58:8 ASV)

Reflection: How would you stand in the gap for those who need you? Are you up for the challenge?

SACRED SPACE

_____

_____

_____

_____

_____

_____

_____

_____

_____

_____

_____

_____

_____

_____

_____

_____

_____

_____

Dear Diary,

Today has been one of those days. So, I needed a Word . . . placed the Bible on the bed and let the pages swing open. And the first verse I noticed was Proverbs 16:25 and I heard You say, "PYRITE." God, that's what you have for me after such a challenging day?

Frustrated, I googled pyrite and came across the Gold Rush of 1849. During this period, numerous people sought "golden" opportunities in the mines of California. Very few hopefuls were successful. Most seekers only found pyrite or fool's gold . . . a crystallized imposter. It looks very similar to the real thing and is often mistaken, but pyrite simply cannot pass the test.

Too often, I find myself in a similar chase. I'm guilty of seeking a quick fix to a long-term problem or hoping for a plentiful return on a mediocre investment. Enjoying the pyrite paradise of my own imaginative accomplishments and living beneath my privilege as a Child of God. We consistently fall for fool's gold and often make conscious decisions to remain there . . . in Pyrite Paradise. Whenever we put our faith in people or things instead of in God, we are only fooling ourselves. I believe that's the warning You were alluding to here in Proverbs 16:25. Many have fallen to Satan's worldly temptations only to learn that the golden opportunity presented was actually pyrite. Like the text suggests, I must be mindful of the snares of Satan and be sure that the way that seems right is of God. I won't be distracted by all that glitters in this world I am willing to be set apart for the glory of God. Only then will I come forth like pure gold.

Focal Scripture: "There is a way that appears to be right, but in the end, it leads to death." (Proverbs 16:25 NRSV)

Reflection: What paths have been a distraction for you? How do you manage those pyrite moments?

SACRED SPACE

_____

_____

_____

_____

_____

_____

_____

_____

_____

_____

_____

_____

_____

_____

_____

_____

_____

_____

_____

Dear Diary,

P = The <u>Prideful</u> . . . Pride is thinking of yourself more highly than another. Those who are prideful find it difficult to see their shortcomings. Usually, they have pretended to have it all together for so long that they actually believe it.

Y = The <u>Yokers</u> . . . A yoke is a bind or tie that holds two things together. These folks feed off of keeping others yoked to their shortcomings because internally, they are still yoked by theirs. The yokers are jokers promoting propaganda.

R = The <u>Ruthless</u> . . . A ruthless person is cruel, callous and calculating. They can't stand to see you happy because they're not happy. Their main objective is to challenge your relationship with God by convincing you that you aren't worth God's grace.

I = The <u>Innocent</u> seem to find themselves in precarious situations often . . . but it is NEVER their fault! But, those who are truly innocent don't have to tell you they are.

T = The <u>Toters</u> . . . Holy Rollers who tote and quote the Bible but don't often display and relay the context in their everyday lives. Toters are often totally out of touch and their interpretation has been based on the lies that they live.

E = The <u>Eager Beavers</u> . . . These are the people that are anxious to tell you what you should be doing but have a harder time heeding God's instructions themselves. Judging and backbiting are very common in this crowd.

Focal Scripture: "And this I pray, that your love may abound still more and more in real knowledge and all discernment, so that you may approve the things that are excellent, in order to be sincere and blameless until the day of Christ." (Philippians 1:9-10)

Reflection: Do you recognize any of these traits in the people in your life? In yourself?

SACRED SPACE

_____

_____

_____

_____

_____

_____

_____

_____

_____

_____

_____

_____

_____

_____

_____

_____

_____

_____

Preservation of a Worshiper

Dear Diary,

I lost two loved ones today. And though death is a very personal experience for many, it moved me to a place I'm not sure I had ever been before. My love for my family is intense and the feeling of community we enjoy when we are together, no matter the cause, is hard to compare to anything else. This revelation reminded me that as a body, our personal relationships with God can be enhanced when exercised through the compassion, love, and support we show one another.

I guess that's why I spent so much of this season mourning . . . not only the loss of my loved ones, but the loss of the false reality that those I thought would stand with me in my time of need would actually return the love and support I had sown. Through it all, though, I realized that even in my time of reflection and loss, God was growing me all the more.

No matter how lost I felt, God, You met me in worship. Our time was preserved beyond my emotion and though the tears seemed endless, You reminded me that I was not alone. It is in seasons like this that I am gently reminded of Your great faithfulness. *"I worship and adore You. I just want to tell You that I love you more than anything."* (Campbell, Lamar. *More Than Anything.* When I Think About You. CD. EMI Gospel. 2000).

Focal Scripture: ". . . Hear my cry, O God; attend unto my prayer. From the end of the earth will I cry unto Thee, when my heart is overwhelmed: lead me to the rock that is higher than I." (Psalms 61:1-2 KJV)

Reflection: What type of loss have you experienced in your life? What elements of growth can be attributed to those occurrences?

SACRED SPACE

_____

_____

_____

_____

_____

_____

_____

_____

_____

_____

_____

_____

_____

_____

_____

_____

_____

Dear Diary,

I saw a tiny little humming bird just outside my window this morning. I couldn't quite hear his song nor did I get to watch him long enough to see the finished product of his tireless efforts, but that bird has been tugging at my Spirit all day!

When birds travel, they tend to stay in formation and remain connected to a group. I have noticed that about a lot of animal species . . . they tend to work together to meet the common goal of the group. They operate in unity to provide protection, obtain shelter and food, and even to train offspring. Animals seem to practice unity among themselves and I know humans could stand to learn a lot from their numerous examples.

I hear You calling us to unity! I know you are urging us to seek harmony and live in peace. Unity promotes the notion that all must agree to walk together. Harmony, then, is the celebration of that unity. It allows one to appreciate individuality, while rejoicing in the accomplishments of a unified community. Musically, even the total measure of a band is best interpreted by a listener who is not confined by the arrogance of self-serving expression, but can appreciate the harmony of the comradery of instruments who share the same vision. If the elite species of Your creation could only come together in unity . . . join hands or somehow work toward a common goal in humility, You are faithful to hear us. That would be the day!

Focal Scripture: "If My people, who are called by My name, will humble themselves and pray and seek My face and turn from their wicked ways, then I will hear from Heaven, and I will forgive their sin and will heal their land." (2 Chronicles 7:14 NIV)

Reflection: What elements of your life need healing? How would you apply the focal scripture to your journey for securing that healing?

SACRED SPACE

Dear Diary,

I've got to get myself together. David said that sometimes you have to encourage yourself. Well David, it's my turn.

The scriptures are not just sayings! They are weapons! You've got to stop trying to fight these battles with your flesh . . . We are too weak to fight that way. You've got to fight these principalities with your heart, where the Lord takes residence and the Holy Spirit brings all things to your remembrance . . . There, you will remember what weapons to bring to the fight! The breastplate of righteousness. . . The shoes of peace . . . The helmet of salvation . . . The belt of truth . . . The sword of the Spirit . . . LIVE . . . And fight like hell to do it, abundantly!!!

Keep walking in the favor of God without apology!!! People are not prepared for what God is doing in you, so they condemn themselves by putting their lying tongues on you all. But don't you follow them down that path!!! Stand firm, stop wavering! You got this and God's got you!!!

William Murphy says, *"It's already getting better. It's already getting easier. God's already moving on my behalf."*

LeAndria Johnson echoes . . . *"Be not dismayed, whatever betide, God will take care of you. Beneath His wings of love, no longer bound. God will take care of you."*

Focal Scripture: "Commit your actions to The Lord, and your plans will succeed." (Proverbs 16:3 NLT)

Reflection: How do you rebound when the enemy rises up against you? Which scriptures or songs bring you strength or encouragement?

SACRED SPACE

Dear Diary,

I hear You talking tonight, Lord. I can hear You interceding on my behalf, again.

My Friend . . . You are a chosen vessel equipped to accomplish the will of our Father and I rebuke the spirits of doubt, confusion, distraction, unworthiness and procrastination that have taken up residence for so long in your Spirit that you have not even realized how prevalent they have become. I command any evil spirit to loose your mind and your heart so that you will walk in the peace of God, your Deliverer! I counter petition any attack on you, your family, your friends and associates and claim total victory on your behalf.

I know My Blood still has resurrecting power, so I command your Spirit to rise up and take charge of your destiny! I know My Blood still has redeeming power so I command your Spirit to fight boldly against any naysayer, backbiter, judge or critic that attempts to hold you to the shortcomings of your past! I know My Blood still has healing power so I command your heart to line up with the ultimate example of God's love as demonstrated through the gift of Jesus. So that your past hurts will be soothed, lessons will be learned, but the memories will lose their painful sting. Your home shall be cleansed, anointed, dedicated and covered in My Blood . . . the doorposts will never dry! Your life shall be a beacon of light to the lost and your unselfish witness will serve as a testimony of hope and verification to the faithfulness of our God!

Focal Scripture: "I have made you known to them, and will continue to make you known in order that the love you have for me may be in them and that I myself may be in them." (John 17:1-26 NIV)

Reflection: Rest in the safety and security of God's unfailing love, tonight and forevermore! Spend time basking in His glory!

SACRED SPACE

_____

_____

_____

_____

_____

_____

_____

_____

_____

_____

_____

_____

_____

_____

_____

_____

Dear Diary,

For 10 years, I lived beneath my privilege as a Child of God! For 10 months, I learned tough lessons from this unrelenting world! For 10 weeks, I lost sight of the Source of my provision while worrying about things I could not change! For 10 days, I allowed bitterness to cloud my judgment and defer my destiny. For the last 10 hours, I've been consumed by how much I have been called to complete and how the obstacles seem to be increasing every day!

Please don't be like me. I wasted so much of my life ignoring my deliverance by walking in disobedience. But for 10 minutes, today, I obeyed The Holy Spirit and watched cartoons with my kids. The last 10 seconds before they went to bed, these God-given, Itty-Bitty Priests reminded me that; life doesn't have to be measured by the years of mistakes you make, the months of opportunities you've missed, the weeks of uncertainty you suffer through, the days of deterrence you experience or the hours you spend faced with the adversities of life.

Maybe, Kevin III and Caleb were trying to show me in their own way that Samuel's lesson can still bless us today. Obedience truly is better than sacrifice!"

So today, I recommit to Christ's example. Into God's hands, I commit my spirit, I submit my will and I confess my suppositions! I'm available for service! I'm dedicated to His call.

I'm girded for the challenge, packed for the journey and fit for The Kingdom! Today, I obey!!

Focal Scripture: "The thief cometh not, but that he may steal, and kill, and destroy; I came that they may have life, and may have it abundantly." (John 10:10 ASV)

Reflection: Are you living your best life now? If not, how can you change that outcome?

SACRED SPACE

Dear Diary,

Friends come and Go . . . Sisters are forever! Since childhood, my buddies, Jenny Girl and Lucy have been great additions to my life. Lucy had a special way of making everyone feel loved. Jenny Girl was gifted in making everyone feel valuable. We were the three musketeers very early on. These were my very first sister-friends!

We enjoyed talking to each other, so occasionally, we'd take a few liberties and share the latest joke or biggest news. We were gossipers and didn't even know it. But as our friendship grew, our conversations matured, our experiences enhanced our abilities, and our shared love for God's people developed, immensely. We were friendly to those who weren't popular and defended "underdogs" at a moment's notice. We were ambassadors . . . the serenity of which I know I didn't even understand at the time.

Our faith in God and one another have kept us connected, even when the phone calls are scarce or the visits are infrequent. Our bond is genuine and the companionship has helped to heal many wounds. Through this connection, I was urged to press even when things didn't go the way I had planned. These lessons are key in life and in worship . . . and I have had plenty of practice learning to perfect this improvisational craft.

Lucy and Jenny Girl . . . I am forever grateful.

Focal Scripture: "A true friend is always loyal, and a brother is born to help in time of need." (Proverbs 17:17 TLB)

Reflection: Who are the people who motivate you? How do you nurture those relationships?

SACRED SPACE

Dear Diary,

'Momma said' . . . two of the most powerful words in my household! If Momma said it, you could count on it. 'Momma said' was the law and no matter what situation arose, I can always remember what Momma said that I could apply in that situation.

Momma taught me how to live, independently. Momma taught me how to love without words but expressions of kindness. Momma taught me how to be a lady, how to carry myself, how to trust my instincts and how to call on God. If Momma said it, it was good enough for me.

Momma said, "If you make your bed hard, you've got to lie in it." I learned that Momma was right . . . and that I don't like hard beds! Momma said, "If you make one step, God will make two." I tried that out for myself and God continues to open doors for me. Momma said, "If you love yourself, you won't allow anyone else to disrespect what God has put in you." That lesson has made me the woman I am today. Momma said, "You can learn something from everybody; even if it's how NOT to act!" Those words are confirmed, daily, as I meet people from all walks of life, of all races and creeds, and with varying opinions about life! Momma said, "Don't worry about what people say; God is the only One you need to please." That wisdom confirmed my purpose and calling.

Momma, I thank God for you . . . and the lessons you taught me. Thank you for loving me enough to help me become all that God designed me to become. We didn't always agree, but we made it. And for that I appreciate you more than you will ever know!

Focal Scripture: "As iron sharpens iron, so one person sharpens another." (Proverbs 27:17 NIV)

Reflection: Whose wisdom helped you develop into the person you are, today?

SACRED SPACE

Dear Diary,

I just want to say, "Thank You!" Today has been a day of reflection for me and I can see that You sent some pretty amazing women my way. Here are some that come to mind:

You sent Rev. Joan Armstead to breathe the life of confirmation into my Spirit. You sent 'Captain America' to teach me the nuances of single-motherhood and the importance of "Me-Time." You sent 'Gigi' to guide me from bad decisions in love to better decisions in life. You sent 'Bella' to show me what being a "Sister's Keeper" is all about. You sent 'Ms. Melody' to teach me that distance doesn't deter divine relationship. You sent 'Ma Mag' to include me, even when I thought I didn't belong. You sent 'Auntie Ma' to support me even when I thought no one would. You sent 'Nana' to cover me, even when she was stretched further than most. You sent my 'Sergeant at Arms' to cover me on and off the battlefield and teach me that blood is not always thicker than water. You sent 'First Lady' to sow into me . . . teaching me that validation comes from You, alone. You sent 'Mert' to push me to press toward the throne of grace through worship. You sent 'Von' to teach me how to be a bold, honest witness for You. You sent 'Grammie' to teach me that in due season, if we don't faint, we will reap what we sow. You sent Ms. Tinsley to demonstrate finer womanhood before me. You sent 'L'Nora' to teach me how to overcome victimization without sowing bitterness. You sent

'Ma Annie' to show me that no obstacle is too great for You. You sent me 'Millie' and Lisa who taught me the beauty of "The Village". You sent 'Franz' to teach me how to walk in the anointing of Job . . . yet they slay me, I will still trust You! You sent 'Shonia' to witness to me that latter will be greater. You sent 'Pastor-Sis' to challenge me to grow into the Woman of God You called me to be. You sent 'HooHoo' to teach me that confession is good for the soul. You sent 'Brina' to remind me that no weapon formed against us shall prosper. You sent 'Ms. First Baptist' to teach me how to be grateful in all situations. You sent 'Senorita' to encourage me to trust You in every situation. You sent Cameo and Rev. Cheryl to remind me to pray about everything and worry about nothing. You sent Onawa to demonstrate that the prayers of the righteous avail much. You sent the 'Authorprenuer' to show me that obedience to You is its own reward. You sent 'Danni' and 'Smurfette' to show me that love is patient and everlasting. You sent 'The Evangelist' to comfort me, though she could have buried herself in her own dilemmas. You sent 'Neen' to encourage me to keep on living because payday is coming after a while. You sent 'Tie' to demonstrate that we don't just live to survive . . . we are made to empower others to live! You sent Ms. Beverly to tame my crazy. You sent me Ms. Ann who taught me that culture is a gift not to be taken lightly. You sent 'Aunt Lin' to nurture my maternal instincts. You sent me Ms. Joy and 'Z' when I needed their love the most. You sent 'Prophetess Lisa' to protect my destiny before I knew who I was called to be. You sent 'Pastor Tara' to remind me that my gifts are worth protecting. You sent 'Di' to challenge me to put You first in whatever I did and watch You work. You sent me Rev. Coleman who encouraged me to meet people just where they are, even if it means you have to pray all the way there. You sent me 'Jacqui' who reminds me to hide The Word in my heart, always. You sent 'Grandma of the Past' to 'learn me' that there's always room at the table or food enough to share . . . because inasmuch as you do for the least of these, you have done it unto God, Himself.

God, I feel like Kurt Karr . . . *"I've got so much to thank You for. So many blessings and open doors. A brand new mercy along with each new day. You're Jehovah Jireh, my provider. For every mountain. You've brought me over. For every trial, You've seen me through. For every blessing. Hallelujah. For this I give You praise!"*

Focal Scripture: "And Jesus looking upon them said to them, "With men this is impossible; but with God all things are possible." (Matthew 19:26 NIV)

Reflection: Why do you praise Him? What women have blessed you over the years?

SACRED SPACE

_____

_____

_____

_____

_____

_____

_____

_____

_____

_____

_____

_____

_____

_____

_____

_____

_____

_____

_____

_____

_____

_____

Dear Diary,

I can't forget the blessings You have provided me through the men I've encountered on my journey. Some of them that come to mind include:

You sent 'Ghost' to have my back, even when most would consider it forbidden. You sent 'Pastor Rob' to affirm me and commission me for Your service. You sent 'Big Country' to teach me that brothers can love, unconditionally! You sent 'Big Brother' to remind me that blood is not the only way to be family! You sent 'Kiko' to help me, even when it wasn't his responsibility. You sent 'Bobby' to teach me that you don't have to fight dirty to stay in the fight. You sent Tyrone to teach me that to have friends, you must be friendly. You sent Dr. Bond to show me that small, meaningful exchanges can have lasting impressions. You sent Pastor Smith who taught me that pastoring is about your heart, not your platform. You sent 'Wood' to remind me that The Anointing makes the difference. You sent me 'Cuz' who showed me that family matters. You sent me 'T' to remind me that no matter how talented you are, only what you do for Christ will last. You sent me 'Daddy Mervin' to urge me to not despise humble beginnings. You sent me 'Drummond' to teach me that real men listen! You sent me 'Coop' who taught me that giving up is never an option and nothing is too hard for God. You sent me Deacon Tony who confirms for me that we are all in God's care. You sent me 'Pretty

Ricky' who urges me to keep swimming . . . and he'll be at the end of the pool, just in case. You sent me 'Q' to encourage me that some of the best gifts come in unexpected ways. You sent me 'Ant' who pushes me to exceed my own expectations without apology. You sent me Everett who taught me that hugs make all of the difference. You sent me 'Shannon' to keep me on the battlefield. You sent me 'IV' to remind me that you are never too young to seek God. You sent me 'Dean' who encourages me to go wherever God ordains, even when the officials do not extend an invitation. You sent me 'Daddy West' who taught me that real men know Jesus. You sent me The Clantons who encouraged me to set my sights on the things of God. You sent me 'Car Wash' who motivated me to be a woman . . . no matter who's watching. You sent me 'Tirry' who reminded me that it's not selfish to take care of yourself. You sent me The Sivells who taught me that food, family, fellowship and fun are all ministries. You sent me 'Pastor Gary' who taught me that God can also live in Texas . . . so taking risks requires discernment! You sent me Pastor Claiborne who encouraged me to own my anointing. You sent me 'Snookums' who motivates me to be better every day. You sent me 'Boom-Boom" to remind me that I can indeed do all things through Christ who strengthens me.

God, I feel like J. Moss . . . *"There's a praise on the inside that I can't keep to myself. A holler stirring up from the depths of my soul. So excuse me if I seem a little giddy or maybe even strange. Cause praise is the way I say thanks!"*

Focal Scripture: "Walk with the wise and become wise, for a companion of fools suffers harm." (Proverbs 13:20 NIV)

Reflection: What men have blessed you over the years? How have you applied those lessons to bless others?

SACRED SPACE

_____

_____

_____

_____

_____

_____

_____

_____

_____

_____

_____

_____

_____

_____

_____

_____

_____

_____

_____

_____

_____

Dear Diary,

I need to be more careful about sharing everything with everybody before God's appointed time. I'm coming out of an "Isaiah-Moment" in which what is going to come to pass had to be revealed because it's the haters (Herod, Pharaoh, Judas, Etc.) that set us up for our divine deliverance! I'm troubled, though, by my lack of discernment regarding the appropriate timing of prophetic revelation.

I have operated in disobedience for so long that I'm just not interested in going back down that path. But, I can't keep terrifying people . . . prophecy is an unnerving mantle to uphold.

Lord, please teach me how to move by Your Spirit in this role . . . please lead me to appropriate examples to follow . . . please incline my ear to hear Your instructions . . . please guide my heart to perceive Your guidance . . . please help me be obedient without procrastinating, but discerning, nonetheless!

You have called me to come forth delivered from the fear, doubt, pride, shame, condemnation, and conviction of who Men/Women say I am. It's time out for playing games. I have to walk in the authority that You have given me to break up the fallow ground of some of these "institutions" that have been "misappropriating" their resources to mislead, manipulate, maneuver and misguide others, but I cannot do this without You!

Focal Scripture: "Teach me to do Your will, for You are my God; may Your good Spirit lead me on level ground." (Psalm 143:10 NIV)

Reflection: To which role have you been called? How do you overcome the reservations you have about filling that role, if they exist?

SACRED SPACE

Dear Diary,

I dreamed that I was climbing a mountain and no matter how far up I got, the distance to the top seemed to increase. I met all types of situations on my journey, but my progress became harder and harder to assess. The clouds were thicker at my feet with each level gained and my visibility below became more and more challenged. I saw others on my journey, but no one offered any support or assistance. Friendly faces and warm smiles met me at each new dimension, but not one helping hand was extended.

As Dorie from Disney's *Finding Nemo* advises, I believe we are in a season in which we should, "Just keep swimming." As I continued to climb that mountain in my dream, I could hear Dorie's sweet voice empowering me to keep going. It was that pleasant thought that brought me to this revelation.

I plead The Blood over our churches and leaders who press toward the mark of the high calling for the glory of The Almighty! I am encouraged to keep GOING, keep CLIMBING, and keep FIGHTING! We can get weary, frustrated, tired and irritated . . . But we can't stop! Dormancy is not an option!

I know You are reminding me to stay focused today and avoid doubt, ignore depression, slide past condemnation and look beyond past failures! I understand that there may be periods along the way when it will appear that I am all alone, but You are always with mc.

Focal Scripture: "And it shall come to pass afterward, that I will pour out my Spirit on all flesh; your sons and your daughters shall prophesy, your old men shall dream dreams and your young men shall see visions." (Joel 2:28 ESV)

Reflection: How did you overcome a spiritual battle that you faced? Which practices brought you the most relief during these times?

SACRED SPACE

_____

_____

_____

_____

_____

_____

_____

_____

_____

_____

_____

_____

_____

_____

_____

_____

_____

_____

_____

Dear Diary,

I wish I could photograph the cloud I've been in since 7:45 yesterday evening!

There were tiny angels in the aisles and Cherubim at each door and pew. The song of the Seraphim blocked out the chants of the demonic forces that were preparing for warfare. The Glory of the Lord clouds the room even now with blurred accuracy . . . So enchanting that though I feel outside of myself, I can see the staircase clearly! With each step, I feel more and more engulfed by His majesty and consumed by His glory.

Confined by my intrigue, but unable to resume without the careful placement of each foot in the pool of His grace on every stair! Saturated by a new boldness that empowers me to act swiftly in obedient servitude - more so than ever before. Engulfed by the sweet aroma of His essence, but too soothed to cough. Panting in rhythm of the beat produced by the wings of the Seraphim as a mother and fetus grow to a syncopated heart tone.

The swelling of desire for His presence increases like engorging glands at an infant's cries. And at that moment, the voice of The Lord becomes all the more audible and the deep gaze of pursued piety transitions to the humble, submissive peer of unworthiness.

As His train fills the Temple with glory, I find myself still; clenched, and bowed . . . Scripting a symbol of Destination with

His blood in the sand at my fingertips! Smoothly written in repetition with every subtle step taken on my knees to prevent my flesh from forgetting my place before the Almighty One!

In this pale sacrifice of service, I see His blood and I'm reminded that His grace is sufficient for even me. It is in His presence that I have fullness of joy and in His perfect will that I survive. It is in His glory that I rise above every infirmity and in His integrity my countenance is elevated! It is in His eyes that I am beautiful beyond my flesh and in His arms I am provided refuge beyond refute!

And in this 24+ hour cloud, I am Me - - - broken but strong, cast down but not cast out, weak but empowered, exhausted but energized, overwhelmed but enamored, torn but tailored, mistaken but motivated, in my flesh but of His Spirit!

I wish I could describe the cloud I've been in since 7:45 yesterday evening. Better still, I wish you could experience Him for yourself!

Focal Scripture: "Counsel in the heart of man is like deep water; but a man of understanding will draw it out." (Proverbs 20:5 KJV)

Reflection: Sunset . . . Just God's way of showing us that the end of one season can also be as beautiful as the sunrise of the next! With God, all things are indeed possible! What scenes come to mind when you think of who God is to you?

SACRED SPACE

_____

_____

_____

_____

_____

_____

_____

_____

_____

_____

_____

_____

_____

_____

_____

_____

_____

Dear Diary,

Only what you do for Christ will last. Behave unapologetically for being obedient to the Spirit of God! Just be sure that what you do in The Name of Jesus is FROM God and OF God. Only true obedience yields fruit!

Tradition, rituals, and religious practices are exercises that were established to help us remember how to honor God and His faithfulness. But alone, they yield no fruit! Exercising obedience in these seasons is the greatest way to honor God. Performing rituals will not take the place of it.

It was in Samuel 15 when Saul's sacrifice dishonored God because he offered it contrary to God's instruction. Samuel simply reminded King Saul that in his position, the tribes of Israel had an expectation that he would follow God at all costs. Likewise, God expects us to obey His instructions and follow Christ's example.

GOD LOVES US!!! And every time we fall short, God's loving hand of correction helps guide us back to the right path. Conviction is meant to correct, not condemn. When we interact with others, it's vital that we do so with the COMPASSION of Christ.

As we mature in Christ, our obligation to know God intimately increases. Intimacy suggests a one-on-one relationship in which God reveals Himself to us, honors our submission to Him and calibrates us to fulfill the purpose for which we were created!

Focal Scripture: "…What is more pleasing to The Lord: your burnt offerings and sacrifices or your obedience to His voice? … Obedience is better than sacrifice…" (1 Samuel 15:22 NLT)

Reflection: Take time to listen to "Order My Steps" by the Mississippi Mass Choir. Determine what it means to you to "walk worthy" and to do God's perfect will?

SACRED SPACE

Dear Diary,

Today I feel like Israel Houghton . . .

"Here I am to worship. Here I am to bow down.
Here I am to say that You're my God.
You're altogether lovely, altogether worthy,
Altogether wonderful to me!"

The issues I face seem to have so much control over me, at times, but I am here to worship, nonetheless. I've got to make a more conscious effort to remember that in all things, I can find strength in worship. I'm here to worship You, Lord! My King. I'm here to acknowledge that You're my God!

Even though the storms of life seem to be engulfing me, I know who I am and most importantly, WHOSE I am. You have taught me that my strength to overcome adversity, is grounded in my ability to remember Your promises to me. I know that my faith in You is in good ground . . . Your commitment to my sanity, security, and success is genuine.

See, in spite of what the situation might look like, the Bible reminds me of a few things that bring me joy . . .
I am more than a conqueror (Romans 8:37)
No weapon formed against me shall prosper (Isaiah 54:17)
All of my help comes from You (Psalms 121:2)

Your grace is sufficient for me (II Corinthians 12:9)

You can heal me (Luke 8:44)

You have a plan for me (Jeremiah 29:11)

You love me (John 3:16)

And that's why I'm here to worship . . . I'm willing to bow down in adoration . . .

> *"Here I am to worship.*
> *Here I am to bow down.*
> *Here I am to say that You're my God.*
> *You're altogether lovely.*
> *Altogether worthy,*
> *Altogether wonderful to me!*
> *I'll never know how much it cost*
> *To see my sins upon that cross*
> *Here I am to worship.*
> *Here I am to bow down.*
> *Here I am to say that You're my God.*
> *You're altogether lovely.*
> *Altogether worthy.*
> *Altogether wonderful to me!"*

Focal Scripture: "Nay, in all these things we are more than conquerors through Him that loved us." (Romans 8:37 NIV)

Reflection: What literary expression (i.e. song, picture, poem, etc.) reminds you of the time you spend with God? How do you nurture that atmosphere or honor that relationship in that moment of reflection?

SACRED SPACE

_____

_____

_____

_____

_____

_____

_____

_____

_____

_____

_____

_____

_____

_____

_____

_____

_____

_____

Dear Diary,

As I reflect on my life, I realize that my disdain was transformed to messages of eternal hope, intimate joy, and ultimate deliverance.

You reminded me that not all of my loss was negative. I'm now encouraged when I think about the times I lost troubling acquaintances and abusive relationships . . . I was delivered from many unsafe conditions. I lost my fear of walking in God's obedience . . . now I decree and declare The Word in season and out of season. I lost my drive to complain . . . I have decided that in all things, I will be content. I lost my desire to please people . . . I now walk in the confidence that my hope is built on nothing less than Jesus' blood and righteousness.

Some of those who walked away are those from whom I should have run from the beginning. Some of those social and emotional obstacles were sent to make me stronger and now I share Marvin Sapp's testimony "Never Would've Made It":

"I'm stronger, I'm wiser and I'm even better!
I never would have made it without You.
I would have lost it all,
but now I see how You were there for me!"

Focal Scripture: "Consider it pure joy, my brothers and sisters, whenever you face trials of many kinds because you know that the testing of your faith produces perseverance." (James 1:2-3 NIV)

Reflection: Take time to listen to Rev. Paul Jones croon "I Won't Complain." What would be the title of the song that best summarizes your testimony?

SACRED SPACE

Dear Diary,

You have equipped me with the peace that can transform my perception of lack into limitless possibilities. What I lost in the absence of those I assumed would stand with me pales in comparison to the wealth of knowledge I gained through their silence. My desire for empathetic camaraderie was fulfilled in communion with the only true source of hope, Your Son, Jesus Christ!

During this time, I realized that disappointment can be multifaceted . . . Just as it can bring you sorrow and emptiness, it can also induce reflective thought and a heart of gratefulness. Adversity taught me that there is a blessing in each storm, an oasis in every valley, a cure for every heartache and an answer to every prayer. Those reasons alone are enough to worship You earnestly, praise You fervently, and give You the glory that is so richly deserved . . . eternally.

Tye Tribbett says it best in his masterpiece featuring John P. Kee, "My Joy":

"You were there to wrap Your arms around me when my nights were cold and lonely. And when I needed shelter from the rain all I had to do was call Your name. You never let me down, You're always there. You told me all my burdens You will bear. I'll never truly understand Your ways but I understand You love

me and for this I want to say . . . You are my joy! It's because of You I smile right in my storm. Your strength is perfect when I'm weak and worn. Thank You for the love You give to me . . . Your grace and mercy. When all of these trials should make me sad, I will rejoice for You have made me glad. You are my joy!"

Focal Scripture: "Do not grieve, for the joy of The Lord is your strength." (Nehemiah 8:10c NIV)

Reflection: How has adversity brought you closer to God?

SACRED SPACE

Dear Diary,

I wonder how Fantasia made it through the ordeals that fostered the writing of "Lose to Win Again." I've lost economic stability, material things and friends, before. Yet, nothing was as painful as that season in which I lost hope. The gods of my frailties once occupied the place of honor that You deserved. Though depression vexed me, somehow it was during those times that my strength was increased, my endurance was enriched and my faith was enhanced. Only a God like You could turn such a dark season into light.

The losses frame my story . . . they color my grayed past, filter my challenged present and highlight my promising future. You built the frame and reconditioned every board. You painted my history into a testimony of deliverance and survival. You tinted my present with the earth tones of your grace. Even now, You cover me in my sleep, in my travel, in my home, on my job . . . You cover my children, my parents, my family, my friends . . . You cover my health, my heart and my future . . . You are faithful and You are my God. With You, I win! All I am is because of Your love, compassion, strength, energy, grace and everything You are! I have lost a lot, but I never lost Your love. And in hindsight, that's good enough for me!

Focal Scripture: "For I am persuaded, that neither death, nor life, nor angels, nor principalities, nor things present, nor things to come, nor powers, nor height, nor depth, nor any other creature, shall be able to separate us from the love of God, which is in Christ Jesus our Lord." (Romans 8:38-39 DBT)

Reflection: Take time to listen to "Let Your Power Fall" by James Fortune & Fiya (featuring Zacardi Cortez). Record the victories God has won on your behalf and rejoice!

SACRED SPACE

_____

_____

_____

_____

_____

_____

_____

_____

_____

_____

_____

_____

_____

_____

_____

_____

_____

_____

Dear Diary,

BUT GOD!

It is so empowering to have a "But God" praise. I'm overjoyed by the thought that You are the author and finisher of my faith. You have the final say and Your Word says, *"For I reckon that the sufferings of this present time are not worthy to be compared with the glory that shall be revealed in us."* (Romans 8:18) In this text, Paul demonstrated his earnest expectation of things to come and admonished the Church to wait on the manifestation of the promises of God, diligently. To me, this encourages me to consider that what the devil meant for bad is going to be used to show Your glory and manifest Your power for my good! Simply because You can!

Hymnist, Lewis E. Jones penned the powerful lyrics to *"There is Power in The Blood"* in which several substantial points prepare us for that imminent victory:

"Would you be free from the burden of sin? Would you o'er evil a victory win?
Would you be free from your passion and pride? Come for a cleansing to Calvary's tide.
Would you be whiter, much whiter than snow? Sin stains are lost in its life giving flow.

Would you do service for Jesus, Your King? Would you live daily His praises to sing?"

I believe in that power, that wonder-working power, that soul-saving power, that life-altering power, that sanctifying power of The Blood of the slain lamb and risen Savior, Jesus Christ.

Focal Scripture: "Much more then, having now been justified by His blood, we shall be saved from the wrath of God through Him." (Romans 5:9 NASV)

Reflection: What hymn resonates with you? How would you describe the impact of The Blood in your life?

SACRED SPACE

Dear Diary,

God, I'm asking for continued favor in the life of my family as I continue to lift my brother and sister in prayer during this season. I felt You leading me to share with others that You are not absent in illness . . . even in sickness, we can STILL be used by You! My family members suffer with pain, either from physical complications or an emotional dilemma and their condition may mirror a medical nuisance commonly known as "Fibromyalgia."

If you're anything like me, you'll appreciate a little breakdown. **"Fibro"** means tissue or fibers. **"My"** means muscle in medical terms (but in Biblical terms, it means "of the people of God" i.e. "My suffering" refers to the suffering of an entire generation . . . that will resonate with you a little later). **"Algia"** means pain or painful condition.

Using this excruciating muscular attack for reference, I hear The Lord saying that in this season of your muscular suffering or physical ailment, the things God shows you during this time are not only for you, but for the People of God! Even while you seek healing, please walk boldly in your calling to strengthen the Body of Christ! Please don't allow Yesterday's pain to negate the rejuvenating fibers of Today's grace which provide the opportunity for you to experience the joy that Tomorrow's mercies will provide!

TODAY has a lot of power! Today can set the pace for how well you move beyond Yesterday and how much you can envision Tomorrow! Today can make Yesterday a blur and Tomorrow a reality! Today, what looked like a mountain Yesterday can look like a valley Tomorrow.

You are to use this season as a learning period . . . (Read Matthew 11:29). And know that even if you are suffering through Fibromyalgia, Diabetes, Divorce, Homelessness, Unemployment, or some other ailment . . . your painful condition is temporary! You must complete your assignment and use your gifts to edify His people! Philippians 1:6 says "...He who began a good work in you will bring it to completion at the day of Jesus Christ."

We all know that "the story" didn't end with the pain of the Crucifixion! It is the Resurrection, the Living Christ and the omnipotent Father that get the last word and own the rights to the closing scene of your life!

Focal Scripture: "His divine power has given us everything we need for a godly life through our knowledge of him who called us by his own glory and goodness. Through these he has given us his very great and precious promises, so that through them you may participate in the divine nature, having escaped the corruption in the world caused by evil desires. For this very reason, make every effort to add to your faith goodness; and to goodness, knowledge;

and to knowledge, self-control; and to self-control, perseverance; and to perseverance, godliness; and to godliness, mutual affection; and to mutual affection, love. For if you possess these qualities in increasing measure, they will keep you from being ineffective and unproductive in your knowledge of our Lord Jesus Christ. But whoever does not have them is nearsighted and blind, forgetting that they have been cleansed from their past sins. Therefore, my brothers and sisters, make every effort to confirm your calling and election. For if you do these things, you will never stumble, and you will receive a rich welcome into the eternal kingdom of our Lord and Savior Jesus Christ." (2 Peter 1:3-11 NIV)

Reflection: Is God the author of your story? Does your suffering get the last word? Review Tye Tribett's "Everything." Is God your everything?

SACRED SPACE

About the Author...

Rev. Caprichia Smith is a native Virginian and the second of five children born to Deacon Phillip and Mrs. Verna Smith. She was raised in the Shiloh Missionary Baptist Church in Cascade, Virginia. Caprichia was educated in the Pittsylvania County public school system and graduated with honors. She obtained a Bachelor of Arts degree in Interdisciplinary Studies from Virginia Tech and earned a Master of Divinity from the prestigious, Samuel DeWitt Proctor School of Theology at Virginia Union University.

In addition to her ministry of motherhood to two small boys, Caprichia has served in several capacities in music ministry, workshop development and instruction, administration, Christian education and more. Applying her gifts of exaltation, worship, praise, prophecy and leadership have been enhanced since she accepted the call of God to serve as the pastoral leader of First Love Ministries. This endeavor, based on the foundation in Revelation 2, promotes the importance of serving, giving to, sharing with, interceding for and loving others the way that is truly representative of the ministry of Christ. First Love Ministries is designed to support the development or maintenance of the interpersonal responsibilities of Christians to love God, wholeheartedly, and demonstrate that love through authentic, selfless service to one another.

Caprichia's journey also includes the development of a comprehensive relationship network entitled, "Fit for the Palace". It is designed to promote holistic health, spiritual healing and emotional wellness in the context of "fit" relationships with God and others.

Rev. Smith is motivated by one of her favorite scriptures, II Chronicles 7:14, "If my people, who are called by my name, will humble themselves and pray and seek my face and turn from their wicked ways, then I will hear from heaven, and I will forgive their sin and will heal their land."

So, her story continues . . .

To Contact Caprichia...

Email: PastorC@FirstLove-Ministries.com

Phone: 501.777.5575

SACRED SPACE

_____

_____

_____

_____

_____

_____

_____

_____

_____

_____

_____

_____

_____

_____

_____

_____

_____

SACRED SPACE